Thank God I Don't Look Like What I've Been Through

Tanya Shaw Tyus

Copyright © 2016 Tanya Shaw Tyus

All rights reserved.

ISBN: ISBN-13: 978-0692655283 (Tanya Shaw Tyus)

ISBN-10: 069265528X

DEDICATION

I would like to dedicate this book in memory of my love ones. My father – Thomas E. Shaw; My sister – Debora Shaw Jones; and my Maternal and Paternal Grandparents respectively – Louis Ben Peters & Julia Mae Peters; Willis Shaw & Ethel Lee Shaw

SPECIAL THANKS

I would like to take this time to give special thanks to some very influential people in my life. First and foremost, I thank God for all he has done in my life. I would like to also thank my parents, my husband and children; they have really been in my corner!! Without them, I would not have made it this far!!

And to anyone else that has made a positive impact on my life, I would like thank you for your support!!

God always has a ram in the bush because God is an on-time God!!!

Be Blessed

CONTENTS

Acknowledgments

Personal Reflections

LIFE EXPERIENCES (The Best Teacher)

LIFE EXPERIENCES (The Best Teacher) – It's Not About Me

LIFE EXPERIENCES (The Best Teacher) – Baby Steps

PART 1- YOU CAN MAKE IT

Testimony 1 – It Did Not Prosper

Testimony 2 – No Need To Worry

Testimony 3 – Where Is Your Faith

PART 2- DON'T GIVE UP

Testimony 4 – More Than A Conqueror

Testimony 5 – Fret Not

Testimony 6 – God Is Able

PART 3- KEEP THE FAITH

Testimony 7 – Divine Protection

Testimony 8 – Jehovah Jireh – Your Provider

Testimony 9 – By His Stripes I Am Healed

PART 4- GOD HAS A PLAN

Testimony 10 – From Fatherless To Highly Favored

Testimony 11 – God Has The Final Say

Testimony 12 – His Purpose... His Timing

PART 5- YOUR LIFE IS IN HIS HANDS

Testimony 13 – God Forgave Me

Testimony 14 – It's Already Done

Testimony 15 – It's Working Out For My Good

MY INSPIRATIONAL POEMS – UPLIFTING WORDS OF WISDOM

Inspirational Poem 1 – Just Because I'm Smiling

Inspirational Poem 2 – Time 2 Reflect

Inspirational Poem 3 – I'm Still Standing

Inspirational Poem 4 – God's Grace

Inspirational Poem 5 – Faith Is

Inspirational Poem 6 – You Can Make It

Inspirational Poem 7 – Forgiveness Is Key

Inspirational Poem 8 – God Can

Inspirational Poem 9 – The Purpose Of The Storm

Inspirational Poem 10 – Purposed Despite The Pain

Inspirational Poem 11 – Do We Believe

Thank God I Don't Look Like What I've Been Through

Inspirational Poem 12– Am I Being Used

Inspirational Poem 13 – He Wouldn't Allow Me To Give Up

Inspirational Poem 14 – A Woman Of Faith

Inspirational Poem 15– I Believe

Inspirational Poem 16– Success Is My Name

Inspirational Poem 17 – I Almost Gave Up

Inspirational Poem 18 – I Am Healed

Inspirational Poem 19– Looking For Love

Inspirational Poem 20– God Is My Source

WORDS OF WISDOM – FINDING YOUR HOPE AGAIN

SCRIPTURES FOR EVERY NEED – A LIFE TOOL

Personal Reflections

As I sit here and think about all that God has done for me and my family, I realize that I am truly blessed!!!! My life has not always been a bed full of roses. I have endured a lot of heartache and pain. I have struggled with many situations, almost given up hope, but God!!! My parents were also inspirational. They instilled in me the importance of trusting God no matter what is happening around me - and I am still standing!!! If it had not been for God on my side, I don't know where I would be!!!!

Growing up, my parents took me and my sisters to church. We had to participate in the different ministries and programs. My father made sure we understood the importance of God's grace, while our mother always taught us to put our trust in God. Being the middle child, I often took life for granted. Not fully aware of the commitment and discipline that was associated with accepting Christ as my Savior, I made many careless decisions. It wasn't until I experienced the death of my oldest sister that I realized life was not always fair.

Sixteen and now the oldest living daughter, I wrestled with my sister's death. My baby sister was only 12 and although it affected her, she really didn't understand the magnitude of this tragic event. I was bitter, angry, and disconnected from reality. I didn't properly grieve and I was so distraught that I looked for worldly peace instead of everlasting peace. For years, I fell into a deep depression that often took the joy of life out of me. I was searching for relief in all of the wrong places, not realizing that I was crying out for God to deliver me from all of the pain and agony that I had built up inside of me. I wanted relief from life's pressure. I wanted to live in a carefree world. I was just so lost and my actions proved that time and time again.

But despite my life's struggles, God blessed me with four beautiful children. He also blessed me to embrace other kids (and care for them as if they were my own) that are very dear to my heart. There were times, I felt like I wouldn't make it. Sickness struck my body at an early age. I married my middle school sweetheart as well as father of my children. My marriage was less than perfect. I experienced a tremendous amount of heartache. I pleaded with God to take away the pain. During all of this chaos, I was enrolled in college, and had to put it on hold. It was just too much, it was unbearable. My life was unraveling and I felt the bitterness creep in once again to confirm my fate. I never thought I would live to see 24 because my oldest sister was killed at that age. I never thought I would weather the storms of my marriage because it seemed as if everyone was against me.

Yet, the same year I got married, my father passed from a massive heartache. Now, I knew that I would never live to see my kids become teenagers because the enemy had tainted my mind with negativity. I never expected to finish college because it seemed as if I was being punished. In so many ways, I felt like Job, trying to understand how to stand strong in the midst of trouble. My mom told me to pray for strength to go through it instead of asking God to take me out of it. Over the next few years of my life and as I neared the end of my marriage, God placed several inspirational people in my life. One older lady adopted me as her granddaughter and took me under her wing until God called her home. She truly blessed me and I will never forget her. There were also a select few pastors that encouraged me regardless of the distance or my location. They always reached out to make sure I knew that God had a divine purpose for my life. I also met a real good friend that helped me see past my trials and told me that I deserved the best and would make it through. Even now, God has strategically placed people in my life that have ministered to me and kept me focused.

I also met a Pastor and his wife that are very special people and have I been very supportive of me in my most recent struggles. They shared their struggles and helped me to realize that all things work together for the good of them that love the Lord, to whom have been called according to his purpose (Romans 8:28). Almost twenty years later, I still deal with some of the negative vices that haunted me at an early age. The difference now is that, I understand that it's a process that has to be experienced in order for spiritual development to take place.

Back then, I regretted every bad situation that happened in my life. I didn't know at the time that God was pruning me, preparing me, shaping me into the person that he had predestined me to be. I used to beat myself up over silly mistakes, until I realized that no one is perfect. Matter of fact, his word says that all have sinned and fallen short of the glory of God (Romans 3:23). So who am I to think that I shouldn't be tempted or tried in this lifetime when my Savior endured massive abuse and torture for our name sake? Wow!!!Now that's love. And because my parents instilled in me the importance of having a personal relationship with God, I returned to my foundation and found peace despite the turbulent waves in my life.

Ironically, during my most turbulent storms is when he birthed the most intricate parts of my purpose. He saw fit for me to travel to another state to speak about his goodness. I never dreamed of being asked to do that. Who was I? Nobody knew me or my story. What could I possibly tell others? Well, God knew me and he had already equipped me for that very moment. Romans 8:31 says if God is for us, who can be against us. Now, after being led by him to minister to others despite the doubtfulness of my abilities, I knew that when God has given me an assignment, he has also made provision for his vision! He gave me visions of empowerment to bless others not with my abilities alone, but with his direction. I never expected to be able to help someone else in the midst of my trials, but God used my pain to mold me into a living testimony for his divine purpose.

Speaking of Divine Purpose, God has also been my shield – Divine Protection. Recently, I encountered a near death experience. Three of my children and I were involved in a very bad wreck. My SUV flipped five to six times hitting a bridge and landing on its side after slamming into a rail that braced us from a 100 ft drop down a ravine. But God!!!!…… Can you believe we walked away without a scratch!!! No broken bones or anything!!! God is awesome and he spared our lives for a purpose!! No devil in hell can take away my destiny!! I believe that I am being positioned for purpose!!!

Now more than ever, my relationship with God is more personal because I have grown through many unbearable life lessons. Just as I gave birth to my children and suffered through the growing pains of childbearing, my learning experiences are filled with many growing pains as well. For He tells us that our suffering is only for a moment, temporary (2 Corinthians 4:17); thus we must continue to look to the hill from whence all our help cometh from (Psalms 121:1). Through it all, I have developed a deeper appreciating for God's grace and mercy. Because of His love for me, He allowed my mistakes to be rerouted into my future successes. All of the pit stops and detours that I took didn't discourage God or make him give up on me; instead he just orchestrated my mishaps and setbacks into setups and comebacks.

As of today, I have completed college and now hold two masters degrees, when I only expected to get my bachelors. My children are blessed and striving as well, despite the divorce from their father. God has also sent me a devoted husband, someone that loves me the way God intended and for that I am grateful. I no longer have uncertainties about my health, God is healing me daily. To God be the Glory!! I even started my own outreach ministry/consulting firm called T.A.N.A which stands for Taking A New Approach (specializes in Education, Business, Youth

Mentoring and Motivational Speaking). What I am saying is, despite all of the bad breaks and agony that I endured, God saw fit to keep me in perfect peace as long as I focused on him. He didn't say the weapon wouldn't form, but he did promise that it would not prosper (Isaiah 54:17). Now I know that the enemy wanted to kill, steal and destroy me, but God saw fit for me to have an abundant life (John 10:10). That is why I must continue to renew my mind with his promises because the enemy is doing his job of making sure I lose sight of God's favor on my life.

There are so many other blessings that I could share with you, but it's not at all about me but about God's amazing grace and how he kept me from destruction. How he allowed me an opportunity to come back to his warm embrace after I strayed away. How he can do anything but fail and can turn your failures into success.

God cannot lie and his word will not return unto him void (Isaiah 55:11). If you don't get anything else from this book, know that if God allows it, he will take care of it!!! His thoughts are not our thoughts and his ways are not our ways (Isaiah 55:8).

Therefore we cannot fathom the plans that he has for us, but we must know that his plan has an expected end (Jeremiah 29:11). And so, I am a living witness that God will give you double for your trouble (Isaiah 61:7). Everything that was taken away, God is restoring back unto me and it's nothing but the Grace and Goodness of God (Deuteronomy 30:3).

The rest of the passages will depict other inspirational accounts of everyday people like me and you and how God brought them through too. I don't know about you, but Thank God I don't look like what I've been through!!!!! Be blessed!!!

LIFE EXPERIENCES:

THE BEST TEACHER

- **PSALMS 119:125**

I [am] thy servant; give me understanding, that I may know thy testimonies.

It's Not About Me

Can you remember the days that everything seemed perfect? No worries and no cares. It seemed as if you could do whatever you wanted to do. But then life happened!! What was that?

Where did all the fun go? Was I being naïve or what? Life couldn't have these many twists and turns or could it? Well, let me help you understand what took place. You see, when all seemed fine, I was being naïve and not really paying attention to life happening all around me. This type of mentality is called selfishness. Everything revolves around me!!!

I guess your next question is: Why didn't God stop me or warn me? Well, I'm almost certain he did show me a sign or two, but I was blinded by my own ambition to live my life as I saw fit. And trust me – all of us have been there. But now that I realize that some changes needed to be made and I have taken ownership of my actions.

Thank God I Don't Look Like What I've Been Through

God is not going to make me change, but will help me along the way. It is not God's job to get my attention. Instead, it is my job to pay attention to him. And now since my focus has shifted for the better, life seems to be more complicated. But it is all a part of God's perfect plan for my life. You see, nothing worth having is easily obtained and I know that this journey called life is not a walk in the park. So I just keep pushing forward while seeking his guidance and now I can see past what I want and move toward his will for my life. Right now, this very moment, I am beyond blessed and I owe it all to God for showing me that's it's all about him and not about me!!!!!

BABY STEPS

What memories do you recall as a baby? Crawling on the floor? Being held by your parents? Playing in your play pen or even swinging in the swinger? Whatever that memory may be – the one constant bond we all share is that over a period of time, we have all grown to where we are now. Some of us are teenagers, young adults and even senior citizens. Regardless of our current age, we all have experienced the many steps, life experiences, trials and tribulations it took to reach that point.

Now think about our relationship with God. This also holds true but differs in that our age doesn't determine our spiritual growth. We can be 60 years of age and still be a babe in Christ. You may wonder – how is this so? Well, because spiritual maturity is contingent upon your personal relationship with God. And the longer you deny him – the longer it will take to grow spiritually. However, it is important to remember that it happens in stages just as physical growth occurs. That is why we shouldn't judge others.

Remember the phrase "Don't judge a book by its cover?" That only means that a person's age does not determine their level of spiritual maturity; their relationship with God does. So instead of judging others by your level of spiritual growth – leave that to the Ultimate Judge and continue to be a living example that God can use daily. Continue to seek him to increase your level of spiritual maturity and understanding of his will for your life. And remember that there is always someone else that is further along spiritually than you too – so judge not!!!

PART 1:

YOU CAN MAKE IT

- **ISAIAH 41:10**

So do not fear, for I am with you; do not be dismayed, for I am your God. I will strengthen you and help you; I will uphold you with my righteous right hand.

IT DID NOT PROSPER

Growing up in poverty was not the idea dream of Justin. He had a rough childhood with no way out it seemed. At an early age, he was on his own having to fend for himself. Little did he know that God had bigger plans for his life!! The reality of living in and out of his car and garages, left with nothing but cardboard boxes and a small dose of hope. But one day, he decided to make a change in his life. He began going to church with his grandmother and singing in the choir. You see, Ray had just recently dropped out of school because of hardship. And even though he was ready for a brand new start in life, it didn't seem to come easy. Yet despite the despair Ray showed, his grandmother continued to encourage him in the Lord. She would often tell him, "Justin, when you are weak, God is strong. It's time that you learn how to lean and depend on him for all your needs. He won't let you down!! I am a living witness that God takes care of his own!!!"

As time passed, Justin's faith continued to grow. He began

to see the light at the end of the tunnel. What seemed to be a setback began to look like a major comeback. One day as Justin was helping his grandmother, he overheard a group of men talking about a chance of a lifetime. So, Justin decided to politely intervene and inquire about the opportunity. And wouldn't you believe that God granted Justin access to just one of his many blessings?!!!

Little did Justin know, those men were professional recruiters and had just offered him a chance to showcase his talent. They were in the area looking for individuals just like him. Now keep in mind, Justin had never played before in his life. But that didn't matter because God had already ordained this divine opportunity.

Justin never imagined that an ordinary guy from a small town would get such a great opportunity. But despite his insecurities, Justin's performance mesmerized the crowds as his passion quickly illuminated the hearts of all that watched him. He continued to play until one day; he was faced with a decision that could alter his professional career. Justin had to decide if he would

Thank God I Don't Look Like What I've Been Through

leave and travel the world or stay home, find a regular job, and take care of his children. Well, Justin chose the latter. He decided that his children needed him more. Of course, he was somewhat disappointed that he would not be able to live out his dream. Yet, Justin never complained about it. Instead, he sacrificed so that his children would have the same opportunities awarded to him.

Justin could have allowed bitterness and selfishness to take route, but he trusted God. And because he trusted God, another blessing presented itself. Justin was asked to mentor to the youth of his community by starting a baseball league. He was such a great influence and role model because he didn't want those kids to give up on life. Justin often shared his story with them, giving them hope to keep fighting despite life's hills and valleys.

Today, Justin still fascinates people with his God-given talents and baseball is not the only one. God saw fit to mold him into a mentor for other young men dealing with similar challenges.

Regardless of the many obstacles that Justin endured during his childhood that could have destroyed his faith, he embraced the spiritual guidance that his grandmother had instilled in him. He is a prime example of divine favor and intervention. For the bible tells us that even though the weapons may form, it shall not prosper (Isaiah 54:17).

How many times have you been faced with difficulties? Maybe like Justin, your childhood memories or upbringing was less than perfect. But that doesn't mean that you can't make it. God is faithful and if he can see Justin through, I know that he will do the same for you!!!!

NO NEED TO WORRY

Imagine marrying your high school sweetheart and enjoying your family. That sounds too good to be true. But this one couple experienced that very thing. Growing up during the most difficult times, especially when discrimination was very prevalent and schools had not been integrated, this couple could have given up hope. They married young, the young man was 22 and she was 18. They would go on to have three children, build a beautiful home and live a successful life despite their upbringing or societal indiscretions.

Lance worked hard to provide for his family, taking courses in college to propel him into the business arena while his wife worked diligently to care for the family. Both of them had decent jobs and supported one another. Of course, they experienced difficult times. I'm sure there were times that they wanted to give up, but because of their foundation in Christ, they weathered the storms of life together and stood on God's promises for their life. Matthew 19: 6 says therefore what God has joined together, let no man put asunder.

This couple had many rocky trials and many uncertain snares to attack their faith, but because they were rooted in his word, God saw them through each battle victoriously. And even though they experienced the loss of a child, God kept them strong. For 36 years, this couple enjoyed the favor of God's blessings. They in return shared their blessings with others. But on one Saturday morning, God saw fit to call her husband home. Now, for years Hope was use to him being in charge of everything and had no earthly ideal how she would cope with his loss. Searching for strength, God answered her prayers.

You see, this woman always prayed without ceasing. She always believed that God would see her through any situation. She had the faith of a mustard seed and God sent her comfort. That very day, after getting back home from the hospital, God instructed one of her daughters to give her this scripture, "Be careful for nothing; but in everything by prayer and supplication with thanksgiving make your requests be made known unto God. And the peace that surpasses all understanding, shall keep your hearts and minds through Christ Jesus (Philippians 4:6-7).

She framed this scripture and still today, it sets on her mantle in plain view so that she will remember how God gave her peace in the midst of her sorrow. Now she is handling every aspect of her life with God's direction. Even though she lost her husband, God sent her a comforter…..the Holy Spirit to be her guide.

In addition to his comforting spirit, God showed his favor on her life in a mighty way. She had no idea that her husband had touched so many lives during his journey on earth. But during and after his home going celebration, people flocked to give her monetary gifts, spoke highly of his charitable spirit and all that he had done for the community. His home going service was packed with people expressing their condolences. Many dignitarians and county officials were in attendance and presented her with a plague. This too seemed to ease her sorrow.

For Hope there were many acts of benevolence on behalf o Lance that she was not aware of until he passed. She was in awe with the generosity and sympathy that was shown to her during her time of bereavement. This made her grateful to have been graced with his love for three decades. Ain't God Good!!! He took her moment of sorrow and used it to bless her tremendously. As a result, she is stronger and understands that God is still in full control!!!!

WHERE IS YOUR FAITH

So many times we allow our doubts and fears to override our faith in God. We know that he is able, but we often dwell on the negative aspects of life instead of focusing on the author and finisher of our faith!! Faith is exactly what this young lady needed as she had a fear of flying.

One sunny day, this young lady had been given the opportunity to take a trip. She was very excited about going, but the only problem was that she would have to fly. Well, Kyndal was very skeptical about flying because this was doing a time that many airlines combined were having glitches in their systems causing numerous crashes.

Every time Kyndal turned on the news, another plane had

fallen from the skies. You can imagine that she was very devastated with the course of events regarding the plane crashes. Her mother was adamant about her cancelling the trip. But still she had a nudge deep down inside that she should go. After weeks of contemplating about the trip and getting advice from her love ones including her husband, she decided to pray about it herself.

She really wanted to go and didn't want festering doubt to keep her from enjoying life to the fullest. The next day, she woke up with a new attitude. She was going on the trip!!!!!!!! What happened? Let me tell you what happened, God gave her peace about her situation. God challenged her to activate her faith and allow him to order her steps. She was distraught and confused because she was fighting fear without the proper ammunition. But God has not given us a spirit of fear but of power, and of love, and of a sound mind (2 Timothy 1:7).

Just the day before she was schedule to leave another plane crash was being broadcasted on every station, but she was determined to still go. She went on her trip and enjoyed herself and went she returned, many asked her what changed her mind.

She politely told them that God spoke to her and said, "If I can take care of you on the ground, I am the same God that will take care of you in the air." And from that very day, she refused to allow fear to overpower her faith in God because she knew he was with her every step of the way!!

PART 2:

DO NOT GIVE UP

- **JOHN 14:27**

Peace I leave with you; my peace I give you. I do not give to you as the world gives. Do not let your hearts be troubled and do not be afraid.

MORE THAN A CONQUEROR

Romans 8:37 tells us that we are more than conquerors through him that love us. What does that really mean? Well, it means that regardless of life unexpected roadblocks, we can still conquer any feat with Jesus Christ!!!! We don't have to experience defeat or despair. We don't have to give up on our hopes and dreams because it seems impossible. For it is written, that which is impossible with man is possible with God (Luke 18:27).

Likewise, we all go through disappointments in life. We even get sidetrack with the plans that we have for our life instead of embracing God's purpose for our lives. Unfortunately, this young athlete had to learn this at an early age. Growing up with an athletic background, her parents were great athletes and her siblings were blessed with that same talent. But this young lady had great aspirations to play for a division one college one day.

Well, her father had the same opportunity in high school but because of injuries, his career and hopes to play on the collegiate level was shattered. Her father was known for his athleticism and had been heavily recruited by many scouters, but after his injuries, he just gave up on life. You see, all his life, he had dreams of being a professional ball player. He never expected to experience a devastating blow to his athletic career.

Now, his daughter was getting a chance to fulfill her dreams and her parents' hopes as well. She was very talented, getting the much deserved recognition that she had worked so hard for. But, ironically every year of her high school career, she suffered an injury. She was devastated, having suffered two of the same injuries that her father had suffered. She wanted to give up and just wallow in self pity, but her mother reminded her that God can still work it out for her good.

Amazingly, Grace decided to stand on God's promises for her life. Those many inspirational words that she had received during her setback kept her focus. Of course, she could have given up hope like her father because of bad breaks, but instead, Grace decided to break the curse of disappointment and loose divine favor in her life.

Although, she will not be able to play a first year of college, she has been given an opportunity to play the following year if she decides too!!!! She is ecstatic about going to college as she plans on becoming a physical therapist. And then Grace can pay it forward by sharing encouraging words of hope (just as she received) with other athletes dealing similar situations. God makes no mistakes, and now what she thought of as a mess of her dreams has now been turned into a message to empower others. This is one of Grace's many testimonies, and is not based on her bad breaks, but it is sparked by her belief that God would work it out for her good!!!

FRET NOT

We all have experienced vices and difficulties on our jobs that caused undue stress. No matter how many times, you've changed jobs, trouble seemed to find you. So what do you do when you are being mistreated on your job? How do you handle favoritism or even jealousy? Well, this one couple found a way to endure biasness in the workplace. They decided to trust God even in the midst of adversity.

The Cantons had been blessed with a great family and jobs. They were prospering beyond measure until a major distraction surfaced on the young Jessica's job. She had been with this company for several years and was working her way up to management. Yet, because of her success, jealousy reared its ugly head. Pretty soon, her boss would try her promotion without any justification. (But we all know that no one can block God's blessing for your life). Imagine working diligently and being denied a promotion only to be asked to train someone that was given the opportunity over you because of jealousy and favoritism.

That is a real hard pill to swallow, but it happens all the time. Even though Jessica was agonized by the unfair treatment, she kept the faith. Good people are not exempt from bad breaks. God's word says that he maketh his sun to rise on the evil and on the good, and sendeth rain on the just as well as the unjust (Matthew 5:45).

What that means is that God has no respector of persons (Acts 10:34). He loves us all but wants us to allow him to fight our battles. And that is just what this young lady did. She did not give up on God. She did not get bitter and retaliate against her enemies. Instead, Jessica and her husband went to God for guidance. One evening, as they discussed some of the unfair practices at her job, God spoke to her husband.

He instructed her husband to get the Bible and open it up. But before Josh did so, he told his wife that whatever passage they open up to and read was God's answer to her situation. Josh opened the Bible and scripture jumped right off the page at them. And they read it together saying, "Fret not thyself because of evildoers, neither be thou envious against the workers of iniquity. For they shall soon be cut down like the grass, and wither as the green herb. Trust in the Lord, and do good; so shall thou dwell in the land, and verily thou shalt be fed" (Psalms 37:1-3).

I am certain that they read the entire passage and receive further confirmation of God's divine protection from all harm. Psalms 37:7 says to "rest in the Lord, and wait patiently for him: fret not thyself because of him who prospereth in his way, because of the man who bringeth wicked devices to pass".

Wow!!! That gives me a sense of peace just reading it!!! It's amazing how God's word can bring peace in the midst of a storm!! It encourages us to *"fret not"* for misfortunes and wrongdoings because he has already orchestrated our victory if we trust him. And that's exactly what he did for this couple. They gave it to him and he delivered them in due season. It wasn't in a week or a few months, in fact it took years for God to manifest their deliverance in the natural realm. But their faith in God never wavered!!!

Today, that same young lady has witnessed some of her oppressors removed from that company while others are still there but have been demoted. However Jessica went on to make top level management!!! Praise God!!! Plus, God blessed her to retire ten years before her retirement age and she has been enjoying it ever since!! Again, God used her oppression to put her in divine position to be blessed beyond measure because our God is faithful and if he said it, then that settles it!!!!! And God can do the same for you!!! All you have to do is stay faithful and trust his plan!!!!!

GOD IS ABLE

Lauren grew up believing that God would take care of her just like the rest of us. But what makes her testimony so special is that God allowed circumstances to strengthen her faith in him. Lauren and her husband of seven years were going through a difficult time. Thomas had just been laid off and bills were piling up. Meanwhile, Lauren was long overdue for a raise at her job, but had not even been considered for one in several years. Her two children were in need of school supplies and everything that could go wrong did. What was Lauren to do? She had been praying and fasting for months and it seemed as if her bills were still piling up and her finances were becoming scarcer. Lauren didn't know what she was going to do.

She began praying relentlessly and believing that God would show up. But still no relief came. One day, she was opening up her mail and realized that her utility bill was overdue and it was $956.76 because they were making partial payments enlight of her husband's unexpected layoff. What were they to do?

The notice said that they had approximately five more days before their services would be disconnected. Lauren had about $300 but they needed food and she needed gas to get back and forth to work. Her next pay check was in two more weeks. She called the utility department and they would not extend any more time because she was already considered three months delinquent.

That Sunday, she went to church and paid her tithes as usual, but in her spirit, she was dreading Tuesday morning. Tuesday was the fifth day and she did not know what would happen. She had prayed before calling to get an extension, but her prayer was not answered. It seemed as if God was so far away. Lauren was distraught and tried to remain in faith even though it was hard to not panic.

But something miraculous happened Sunday at church, God sent her a word. That word was….. Ephesians 3:20 " Now unto him who is able to do exceedingly abundantly above all that we ask or think, according to the power that works in us." Lauren and her husband received this word and almost immediately…..their burdens were lifted. God reconfirmed that he was always with them, even in the midst of the storm. He reassured them that he would take care of the situation in his own way and time.

Tuesday came and went, but their lights were still on even into the following week. And then, two weeks after the disconnect notice, their new bill arrived and it showed something miraculous. Instead of it showing the past due amount with the current amount, it showed just the current bill due. For some odd reason, the past due amount on the statement of $956.76 had been paid!!!

Lauren immediately called the utility company to check on it and the representative told her that it had been paid on Tuesday in full. Jessica couldn't understand how because they had not paid it and nobody else knew that they were in need. Now, Lauren was a little worried that it would be found an error and the lights would soon be disconnected. But I am here to tell you several years later that the word God gave them was their debt cancellation confirmation!!!! God did exceedingly, abundantly above what they could even think or imagine!!! And God is willing to do the same for you and me!!!!

PART 3:

KEEP THE FAITH

- ### DEUTERONOMY 31:6

    Be strong and of good courage, do not fear nor be afraid of them; for the Lord your God, He is the One who goes with you. He will not leave you nor forsake you.

DIVINE PROTECTION

As parents, we try our best to take care of our children to provide for them and keep them safe. Well, God does that for each and everyone one of us. We are his children and he keeps us and blesses us despite our faults. But, this mother of four didn't really understand how blessed she was until she saw God's hand in her young daughter's life.

One sunny day, Kandice was headed to her parent's house to pick up some home cooked food that her father had prepared for his grandbabies. Kandice's mother opened the door and all of the kids jumped out of the car except the two baby girls. Kandice wasn't in the house but a few seconds just long enough to grab the food and head out of the door. But when she approached the door, she saw her car rolling down the drive way. How could this be? Kandice had her keys in her hand but noticed Renee in the driver's seat and Nicole trying to get out of the passenger door. It was so horrific to see her youngest child being run over and dragged to the bottom of the driveway.

Kandice panicked, but as she was about to pass out, her father pulled up and had witness the entire accident as he was approaching the house. Baby Nicole had laboured breathing and her head was distorted from the impact. She had blood all over her and the family was in tears. She was rushed to the nearest hospital where she was flown to a trauma center for children. Miraculously, she recovered without any problems. Yes, she still has a scar to remind her of God's divine protection, but today she is a thriving young lady!!! This child had already defeated the odds by being born premature and being sick most of her infancy. And for this to happen when she was only eighteen months further proved that God had a plan for her life.

Now, she is a freshman and a great athlete and student. She is very ambitious and thanks God daily for keeping her in safe in his arms. She understands his divine protection and shares her story about the scar of God's love that people often inquire about. God is good!!!!! And he surely did reinforce the meaning of

Divine Protection to Kandice!!!! Won't God take care of his own!!!! Yes he will!!!! Divine protection!!!! I believe he says…."Touch not my anointed (1 Chronicles 16:22)!!!!" Praise God and know that he will protect his children because he is such a Loving Father!!!

JEHOVAH JIREH-YOUR PROVIDER

How many of us truly trust God to provide for us? When our finances get crazy, our jobs expire, and our change gets strange? Do we know beyond a shadow of a doubt that God will work it out? Or do we possess doubting faith- you know that type of faith that is intercepted by doubt. For Melinda, she was experiencing doubting faith because she had been unemployed for almost a year. But something miraculous happened for Melinda!!!! God made provision!!!!

Let me share her testimony with you about how God made provision. Melinda was a licensed attorney that could practice in several states. She was highly qualified and highly favored, but just as soon as her blessings began to flow- they came to a screeching halt. Was it something that she did? What was going to happen now? Well, the law firm she was working for went out of business, leaving her unemployed in that state with no family.

Melinda quickly decided to move back to her home state and live with relatives until she could find employment. She was optistimic because she was a licensed attorney and just knew that her unemployment would be short lived. Unfortunately, weeks turned into months that ended up being a little over a year. No income coming in and frustration setting in because she had to depend on family.

Melinda found herself sinking into a deep depression. She prayed and prayed but felt as if God was ignoring her request. She was turned down for jobs for being over qualified despite the fact that she would take lesser pay just to have a form of income. After all the disappointment from not finding a job, Melinda decided to give up and called her best friend to wallow in self-pity. But I guess Tanya didn't get the memo because she stepped all over Melinda's toes!!! Tanya told her that God had given her the ability to make ends meet, but she was not stepping out on faith.

Melinda complained that she didn't have the resources to start her own business and couldn't afford a building. Still Tanya insisted on working on a business plan, looking for office spaces and advertising her services as well. Yet, Melinda was skeptical about this type of Faith Walk……but she decided to do it anyway.

Another month passed by and it seemed as if nothing was happening after stepping out on faith and moving forward to start her own business. Melinda once again began to feel down. Little did she know…..God was working behind the scenes? Melinda got a phone call from the Public Defender's office in her county about a possible job. Over the next few weeks, more and more clients needed her services and within a month of building her clientele, she secured a building.

Today, almost seven years later, her business is still thriving and she is well respected in her community and surrounding areas. God provided her an opportunity to step out of her comfort zone through the most uncomfortable situation and experience his abundance. God wants to do the same for you!!!! He is your provider…….not your job or your spouse!!!! God is Jehovah Jireh……..our Provider!!!! And every need we have God is faithful to provide in his own way and time!!!!

BY HIS STRIPES I AM HEALED

Imagine giving birth to healthy children and not knowing that sickness would strike your son's body. This is what happened to the Sangsters' as they witnessed their son become ill time after time with no relief. For Charlotte, she was a stay-at-home mom that believed in the healing power of Jehovah Raphi. But month after month, her son was either visiting a doctor or hospitalized with debilitating headaches. Further evaluation determined that the headaches would worsen with uncontrollable seizing episodes.

The Sangsters' faith did not waiver despite the prognosis. They seemed to be calmer than their other family members during this difficult time. Year after year passed and their son, Isaiah, continued to fall victim to the sickness that had started when he was very young. Now the time had come that he was a few years shy of being a teenager, but his opportunity to enjoy life had been diminished because of precautionary measures decided by his physician due to the sporadic seizures.

Well just a year shy of his thirteenth birthday, Isaiah suffered an unexpected seizure after being seizure-free for almost two years. This time the illness threatened his life. The physician quickly expressed his concerns and explained that surgery would be the best option. Surgery?!!! Wow!!! This was very serious!! The Sangsters had to decide if they would give medical consent to allow a neurosurgeon to operate on their son's brain.

But after much prayer and fasting, the Sangsters agreed to go forward with the surgery. They surrounded themselves with prayer warriors and were constantly feeding off of God's promises for their life. Charlotte had even written a heartfelt letter to her son and put it in her Bible marked Isaiah 53:5 (*But He was wounded for our transgressions, He was bruised for our iniquities; the chastisement for our peace was upon Him, and by His stripes we are healed*). That scripture was where she placed her faith in God to heal her son. She knew the surgery could be risky, but she also knew that God was a divine healer. She didn't allow fear to override her faith.

In the operating room, the procedure didn't go as planned. Isaiah's oxygen level dropped and he was not responding to the antibiotics. But still the Sangsters' kept praying and believing. Almost eight hours later, the neurosurgeon emerged from the operating room with a relieved expression on his face. He informed the parents that the procedure had been completed and they were just watching his vitals before moving him to the recovery room. As he turned to leave, he stated that he was blessed by their unwavering faith even during such a difficult time.

You see, the Sangsters were not having a pity party…….instead they were having a praise session!! They had no idea that the neurosurgeon even noticed their faith. They were too busy giving God the praise for what he was going to do in that operating room. And wouldn't you know that Isaiah made it to the recovery room and to date is doing exceptionally well!! Did I mention that he has not experienced a seizure in almost four years?!!

Now, after reading this …. you must know that God can heal

any sickness!!!! Nothing is too hard for God (Jeremiah 32:27)!!! Whatever it may be: cancer, heart disease, diabetes, hypertension, lupus, or any other illness…..God is a healer (Exodus 15:26)!!!! Give it to God and allow your faith in him give you a peace of mind. But don't let the enemy cause you to give up on your life!!!

PART 4:

GOD HAS A PLAN

- **JEREMIAH 29:11**

For I know the thoughts that I think toward you, saith the Lord, thoughts of peace, and not of evil, to give you an expected end.

FROM FATHERLESS TO HIGHLY FAVORED

Jayson was always a hard working young man. Growing up without a father figure made him realize how much he wanted to beat the odds. After graduating from a small town high school, Jayson immediately went to college. Well, for some reason, he was not as focused as he had intended and dropped out after struggling to maintain his grades.

After getting involved with the wrong crowd and finding himself all alone when he needed his so-called friends the most, Jayson decided to change his life for the better. He applied through a temporary agency to work at a local factory. What was meant to be temporary turned out to be a permanent position that spanned over a decade.

Now Jayson was doing well for himself and those so-called friends resurfaced. But Jayson ignored the valuable lesson that was taught to him before about the company he was keeping. It took another eye opener to get his attention because he was slacking on going to church when he found success again. One day, a life altering announcement was made about the plant closing down. Jayson wasn't too worried because he was a veteran worker and never missed a day of work. However, to his surprise, he was one of the first individuals to be laid off. He was confused! How could temporary workers still be working and he get laid off?

Well, he tried to make sense of it all and felt that his friends would help him through this transition. The once popular Jayson was now a "has been". All of his so-called friends once again left him in his time of need. This time, he took it harder because he considered his friends to be loyal. This broke his spirit and he became depressed. For months, he moped around the house and began to allow his health to dwindle.

In the wake of all the turmoil, he decided after a few years of unemployment to step out on faith. This time in a new direction: a new career path. Well, guess what?!!!! God had his hands on Jayson's life. What the enemy meant for bad…God used it for his good (Genesis 50:20)!!! Jayson started a new job several years ago and within a year was promoted twice on his job!!Praise to be God!!! Now he is second in command and understands that sometimes were God is taking you, everyone can't go!!! Thank you Lord for blessing the many Jayson's around the world and letting us know that it's okay to leave them (so-called friends) where they are because God has a plan for us all!!!

GOD HAS THE FINAL SAY

How many of us have been in situations where we were told no? Did we allow what others thought to determine our path? Did we give up because we met opposition when pursuing a particular goal? Well, I am here to tell you that God has the final say (Lamentations 3:37)!!!! Man may say "No" but if God says "Yes", it is already done!!!! Don't let what others think or say about you cause you to negate your blessings. Instead, keep striving and pursuing your dreams and let God give you the final say!!!!

That is just what Marcy did!!!! She did not allow other people to discourage her dreams. Marcy was a very intelligent young lady and always wanted to go to an academic school. She pleaded with her mother to allow her to enter into a prestigious academic high school with hopes of graduating top of her class.

But this dream was not easily obtained. Marcy was met with immense opposition her first semester.

Coming from middle school as an honor student and now on the verge of being put on academic probation, Marcy was devastated. She became depressed and was contemplating leaving the school. She spoke with her parents and they encouraged her to buckle down, have faith and give it to God.

Marcy desperately tried to forget the piercing words typed on the academic probation notification letter. It read, "We fear that this school is not appropriate for Marcy. We believe that if she stays, she will not benefit from the rigorous courses taught to prepare our students for college". What a discouraging letter to send to a freshman scholar that had just failed one class.

It could have been the transition from middle school to high school. It could have been the increased level of instruction from a school that places emphasis on college preparatory classes. Whatever the case may have been in Marcy's dilemma, sending that letter only deepened her doubts of ever graduating at the top of her class.

Nevertheless, the faith of her parents and grandmother helped Marcy to stay the course. Marcy's grandmother told her, "Marcy, you don't give up!!! You let God do his part and you do yours!!! God has the final say baby!!! And I believe God is going to work it out for you!!" Just those encouraging words from her grandmother helped Marcy to embrace the opposition instead of running from it.

And today, Marcy is thriving and still attending that school. Matter of fact, she is on track to graduate in the top percentage of her class!!!!! So, just remember that God has the final say not people!!! Besides, were would some of the people you admire be if they had given up because they were rejected!!!! Exactly!!!! Because if Jesus had given up on his mission, we would not be able to share our testimonies!!!! Now stay focus and keep the faith because giving up should never be an option!!!!

HIS PURPOSE - HIS TIMING

Ever felt like giving up because it seemed as if your breakthrough would never come? Ever felt so down and out that it felt as if your prayers were not being answered? The truth of the matter is – we all have at some point in our lives. The overwhelming pressures of life sometimes weigh us down. And then we lose sight of our refuge by dwelling on the problems we face. For Kenya, she knew first-hand about losing hope. But it was her faith in God that helped her through her most trying times.

Kenya was a single mother of four beautiful children and she had experienced the effects of a spiraling economy for approximately four years. She would be laid off at her fulltime job, only to find odds and end part- time jobs to tackle her bills. Now, Kenya was very smart and had finished several degree programs that would be an asset to any company that hired her. But unfortunately, her degrees and extensive experience was overlooked by many companies as she enthusiastically searched for employment. Then one day, she was faced with yet another devastating blow. Her part-time job laid her off and she began to draw unemployment only to be in the middle of a congressional debate that ended her benefits.

Kenya was devastated and cried out to God for help. She decided to start back working on a vision that God released to her four years ago that was put aside because she was working at the time. Now she was back where she was started at four years ago: unemployed. For Kenya, it seemed to be a curse. But could it be that God was preparing her to step out on Faith in the direction that he wanted her to pursue? Regardless of the anguish, Kenya did not give up. She continued to seek God for his guidance and worked diligently on the visions he gave her. Even though she didn't find a job, she has never gone without. God made provision for her every time and she believed without a doubt that he will see her through. Kenya now looks back over her disobedience and realizes that her talents and gifts are what God has elevated during this transition to make ends meet. She realizes now that where she is God has to guide her and she has to walk by faith. No more trying to orchestrate her life on her own. For where God has Kenya, she can't go back to where she came from or move forward without God's guidance. She has decided to trust him wholeheartedly as he has shown her his faithfulness during her storm.

Furthermore, we all are guilty of sometimes ignoring God until we are put into a situation where we must listen. And just like Kenya, he will manifest his purpose for our trials and tribulations in due season. He will manifest our breakthrough when he sees fit!! All we have to do is trust his timing and his purpose because he knows best!! So now I ask you…when you are faced with life's uncertainties…..will you trust him?

PART 5:

YOUR LIFE IS IN HIS HANDS

- **ROMANS 8:28**

And we know that all things work together for good to them that love the Lord, to them who are called according to his purpose.

God Forgave me So why can't you

We all have been victims of wrong doing as well as being the deliverer of wrong. But the one thing the victim and the wrongdoer have in common is that God has no respecter of persons. God will forgive me just like he will forgive you. The problem is we often forget how many times we have asked God for forgiveness for our sin. But we are quick to hold others to theirs. Is that right? Should we be biased about who should be forgiven and should not be? Well, for Thomas, he had to endure ridicule of his past just because people didn't find it in their heart to forgive him.

Thomas was very young when he started hanging with the wrong crowd. He had experienced the death of his mother at an early age and didn't know his father. As a result, his grandmother raised him until she passed away when he was fourteen. For Thomas, this was too much to handle. Before this grandmother's death, Thomas was an honor roll student, member of the junior deacon board, and enjoyed volunteering for community service activities. But, after his grandmother transitioned, he decided to stray away from what he was taught.

Thomas was mad at God because he lost his grandmother when he felt he really needed her. He didn't understand why it would happen to her because he watched how faithful his grandmother was to God. One summer day just before his seventeenth birthday, Thomas joined a gang. He was trying his best to fit in and was often the fall guy for many atrocious acts of violence. Time after time, Thomas was in and out of jail faced with assault and robbery charges.

Many of his grandmother's church family began to reach out to him. One time, they even posted his bail with the stipulation of him coming to church on Sunday and bible class on Wednesday. For awhile, Thomas was doing great, but his gang affiliation quickly halted that agreement and he was back at gangbanging hard. Unfortunately, it appeared that he was lost and that the streets would either bury him or lock him up for life. But God had a plan!!! For he always had Thomas in the palms of his hand.

Even though Thomas had strayed away, he still prayed every night for God to help him find peace. And little did he know; God was orchestrating his breakthrough every time he prayed regardless of how he was roaming the streets. On his twentieth birthday, Thomas was arrested on an armed robbery charge. This was a major blow because he did not commit the crime but was set up by some of the guys in his gang.

Thomas was devastated and fell to his knees while in the holding cell. He was so used to posting bail but never expected to be held without one. Now, Thomas had to await his trial that was sixty days later with no clue of how he could defend himself. They had his gun and apparently one of his friends used it in the robbery and no fingerprints were found except his.

Thomas began to pray day and night. He asked God to show him the way. He asked God to forgive him for his wrong doing and for still blessing him despite his sin. A month before the trial, Thomas had a dream. God told him that once this situation was behind him, that he must turn from his ways and follow him again. Thomas was scared because of his gang ties, but willingly agreed. God then told him to not be afraid, for if he is for him, he is more than the world against him (Romans 8:31).

The day of the trial, his lawyers found some loopholes in the prosecutor's case and as a result, the case was declared a mistrial. Thomas was so elated!! He fell to the floor and began to thank God for his deliverance. As Thomas was preparing to be set free, he heard a voice say, "forget those things which are behind and pressed toward the high calling" (Philippians 3:13-14). Thomas knew exactly what he had to do. He relocated to an area near some of his relatives and began connecting with God. You see, Thomas was a very gifted singer that only song one time and that was for his grandmother's home-going service.

However, for some reason, he felt the urge to write lyrics of about his life. He even reconnected with a former classmate that was musically talented as well as a producer to put his words to music. It was a success, but also a major blow to his character. Many people didn't want to forgive Thomas for his past or even give him a chance. They felt as if he had done too much and he was just trying to manipulate people to make a financial gain.

But, their judgmental views were wrong. God had redeemed Thomas!! God had saved and restored him. And despite the backlash from his past, God saw fit to make him an up and coming recording artist while his enemies were somewhere watching him succeed. God can do that very thing for you too!!! Our mistakes don't cause God to abort his purpose for our lives!! Sometimes, it takes for us to get drenched in our mess to understand God's love for us. Our mess becomes our message, our test becomes our testimony!! For, we all have sinned and fallen short of the glory (Romans 3:23). Plus, we all need God to forgive us daily and cleanse us from all unrighteousness. And regardless of who decides that they will not forgive you, God does and that's all that matters!!!

IT'S ALREADY DONE

How many times have we prayed about something and it appeared that nothing was happening? At least not in our minds anyway, right? But it is important to remember that God never allows us to go through anything that will not benefit us in the end (Jeremiah 29:11). With that in mind, we must stand on His promises. We must also remember that our ways are not His ways and our thoughts are not His thoughts (Isaiah 55:8). And in due season, whatever it is that we are praying for as long as it is in God's perfect plan, it is already done (Matthew 21:22)!!!! We just have to believe by Faith to receive it in the natural!!!

For Casey, this was a real challenge to stand on faith for seven years believing God would increase his business. Casey had experienced his bout with being underemployed for seven years. He was very well versed and educated and also willing to acquire the necessary skills needed to find decent employment in the workforce. But God had other plans for Casey that did not include the average 9 to 5 job. Casey knew deep down inside that his calling was to be more than just average. Yet, Casey continued to avoid it by chasing jobs that never seemed to fulfill that passion bottled up on the inside.

Sometimes Casey would pray for a better job and would wonder why he was never called for an interview. Or he would get upset because the interviews would go well, but the job offers would never follow them. Have you ever felt this way? Have you ever been in a situation similar to Casey? Of course, this can get frustrating, but Casey forgot one important thing. He never stopped long enough to ask God "what is it that you want me to do"? All Casey did was pray for God to do something for him. Every prayer was a request for God to bless Casey. To be honest, Casey was being very selfish!!

This gives you a different perspective now doesn't it? You see, Casey was being disobedient and wanted to be blessed to do what he wanted to do. He wanted to accomplish what he wanted to accomplish. And he never considered stepping out on faith for what God had predestined for him to be. This is similar to Jonah and his rebellious spirit. But, it would not take Casey long to figure out of his ways and thoughts were not what God had for his life.

The following Sunday morning, after numerous job searches and no offer in sight, Casey decided to go to church. He arrived with a spirit of heaviness and confusion because he was wrestling with what his first mind had told him to do. To Casey, it did not make since to start his own consulting firm. He was unemployed, no income, no building, and definitely no idea of what a consulting firm would entail. So to Casey, this had to be the enemy's tactic to put him in a bind.

Nevertheless, as those thoughts raced through his head, the song *"Break Every Chain"* was being sung. It began to minister to him and tears began to flow. After a few selections, Casey was eager to hear the sermon. As the pastor took the pulpit, he referenced his scripture and gave the title of his sermon, "In God's timing it's already done". Casey couldn't believe his ears!!! It was like the message was designed specifically for him. The pastor went on to say that God has a perfect plan for our lives and that we have to be obedient and walk in it by faith. He reiterated that it will not make sense to us because God's plans are bigger than our minute minds. So much so that we cannot even fathom the many blessings that he has for us (Ephesians 3:20)!!!

Casey left church with a new perspective and the willingness to step out on faith. After all, God had been sustaining him for seven years without a job and he was still making it!!! A month after that life-changing Sunday, Casey opened up his consulting firm from home. His consulting firm was unique because he was helping youth find their passion.

Currently Casey is at peace with his decision to follow God's plan. He is doing exceptionally well in his new business because God ordained it from the beginning. And to think, all Casey had to do was ask God to show him his purpose, and just like that, God would have revealed it because it was already done!!!! What about you? Have you asked God to reveal your purpose to you? If so, do not hesitate to step out on faith and be obedient because it will be the best decision you ever made!!!!! Besides, when you believe in God's plan for your life…..everything falls into place. And never forget, ***In God's timing ….it's already done!!!!!!***

IT'S WORKING OUT FOR MY GOOD

Romans 8: 28 tells us that all things will work together for the good of them that love the Lord to whom are called according to his purpose!!! That in itself is a reason to rejoice. Just to know that regardless of what is happening all around us, God is perfecting it and working it out to benefit us. That includes anything that we could ever go through. It could be a loss of a loved one, a divorce, the loss of a job, a foreclosure or repossession of our property, or even sickness. It doesn't matter what the situation is!! It doesn't matter how bad it seems!!! It doesn't matter what the enemy meant for bad because God promises us that it will all work out for our good!!! This is definitely what happened for Jared during a difficult time in his life.

One day, just like every day, Jared was at the gym working out before he went to his corporate job. But for some reason, Jared wasn't feeling like himself. He felt this impending doom and had been feeling that way for approximately two weeks. However, instead of going to the doctor to make sure everything was fine, he decided to brush it off as job stress.

At the gym, Jared decided to call a co-worker and just tell them about how he was feeling to help him dismiss the possibility of anything major. Yet, his co-worker insisted that he go to the doctor just for precautionary measures. Well, of course, Jared did not go. He argued that he was in the best shape of his life and had no reason to feel that his health was an issue. He just assumed that it was stress from the big merger that was approximately two weeks away and that he needed to just relax.

Then something happened!!!! Sirens and flashing lights were fading in and out. White coats and gloves were slightly visible. The more he tried to understand what was happening, the more he drifted into this abyss type encounter. What was happening? Jared was desperately trying to make sense of all of the unexpected events only to learn a month later that he had drifted into a comma from a major stroke. You see, right after he spoke with his co-worker he walked toward the treadmill and started to exercise. And a few minutes later, he was being rushed by ambulance to the hospital.

The deep abyss he experienced was most likely his ability to hear the chaos happening around him, but not being able to respond to it. For an entire month, family and friends prayed for his speedy recovery. And God answered their prayers when Jared opened his eyes. This was a good sign, but he still had a long recovery to endure. Jared had to learn how to talk and walk again. He even had to have brain surgery to remove the affected areas. But, Jared remained optistimic. After eight months away from his family and friends in a rehabilitation facility two hundred miles away, Jared was finally able to come home.

At first, Jared was feeling sorry for himself and ready to get back to life as he knew it. He wanted to rush the recovery process and felt as if he was being unproductive. It was hard for him to grasp not being able to work because he had been in the workforce since he was sixteen. Self-pity began to set in and he became depressed. He started looking through some of the messages sent to him during his traumatic event and decided to reach out to a classmate.

Jared needed to talk to someone about what he had experienced. He wasn't sure who he could trust, but God put on his heart to reach out to Cassi. Cassi began to minister to Jared about how God always takes care of us. She reminded Jared of how blessed he was to be able to regain his memory and activities of his limbs. Jared's perspective began to change and he started seeing his sickness as a blessing. Now I know you are wondering how this could be a blessing? But for Jared, it allowed him to experience God's goodness and mercy on an entirely different level. You see, developing a personal relationship with God is just that......it's personal!!!! Every situation or trial that we experience should draw us closer to God!! And for Jared, he realized that God spared him because he still had work to do!!! It had nothing to do with how healthy he was before. Neither did it have any reflection on his situation after the sickness because God sustains what he ordains. Jared realized that God equips those He calls and what we think we need is totally different from what God gives us. This situation allowed Jared to fully trust God instead of his own abilities. It was definitely a vulnerable place, but simultaneously humbling because Jared learned how to let go and let God!!! He also realized that he could bless someone else that may be going through something similar with his testimony of God's faithfulness.

God is a healer!!!! Jared is evidence of that!!!! Now, he is encouraging others during their trials and tribulations as he continues to improve his health. For those of you that are going through, try to find something good out of your situation. Besides, it could always be worse. If Jared had not opened his eyes to the goodness of God despite his traumatic experience, he would still be encountering that deep dark place of depression. But thanks be to God, because of his faith, God illuminated his hope and gave him joy!!!!

And you can experience that same joy!!! God is able and He is worthy to be praised!!!! We should praise him during the good times as well as the bad times because God is always good to us (Psalms 136:1)!!!!! Let us join Jared in our praise!!!!! Let us give thanks despite our pain!!!! Let us rejoice anyway!!!!! Just because we know that it will always work out for our good if we have faith!!!!

My Inspirational Poems:

Uplifting Words of Wisdom

- **PROVERBS 3:13**

Blessed is the man who finds wisdom, and the man who gains understanding.

JUST BECAUSE I'M SMILING

Just because I'm smiling, doesn't mean I haven't been through.

And just because I didn't break down and cry before you, doesn't mean I haven't been misused.

Yes, you may think I'm conceited, stuck up, and even despise me

But what you really envy is the God in me

I can't control how you feel or what you think about me

I can only control my thoughts and my actions that affect my destiny

So don't waste time thinking that your pettiness will succeed.

Because I serve an Almighty God and he will protect me.

And even though you formed a weapon against me

My God promised that it would not prosper against me.

Yes, I'm blessed and I'm walking in my victory

This is my season of unexpected blessings and I receive thee.

So my smile is evidence that my God has kept me along the way

And my smile is confirmation that he will elevate me despite adversity along the way

My smile is the joy that I have despite the heartache and pain

Thank God I Don't Look Like What I've Been Through

My smile symbolizes the shining sun that comes out after the rain

Oh yes, I'm blessed and smiling from ear to ear

I'm smiling and at peace because my God is real

You see I'm smiling because everything I have God has given to me

I'm smiling because I am thankful, and I didn't deserve anything

But the main reason, I smile is because of God's goodness and his grace

And that's why for as long as I live, I will lift up his name in praise.

TIME 2 REFLECT

What does life mean to you?

Is it to gain worldly things-While satisfying every insatiable need?

Or is it to live a life for Christ

Exemplifying his spirit that is within?

Spreading his goodness to family, foes, and friends

Recognizing that he holds all power and it's his grace and mercy

that we dwell in

Daily he breathes blessing over us

To protect us from all harm

That we may be living witnesses of his extraordinary presence

Not taking anything for granted: for life is not promised

Nor can we extend favor with ourselves

Yet we are helpless beings-passing through phases of the unknown

Hopefully forgetting those things which are behind and pressing

toward a higher calling from his radiant throne

So what do we do to show our service to our Savior, the one who

set us free?

Do we yield ourselves to him totally or entangle ourselves in

selfish captivity?

It's a time to reflect: a time to adhere to his perfect plan. Truth be told, we can't waste another minute procrastinating. For so many

years, we have tried to manage our own fate. Wasting time and

concocting deadly schemes along the way. Breaching the

inevitable contract set before us at birth.

Struggling to find our inner worth: but not by birthright because

our predestined plan has already been designated. How then can

we claim to be righteous in our own thinking? Condemning one

another- always judging fellow sisters and brothers

Masquerading behind an illusion of pride that delivers us into a

condemned place full of deceit, selfishness, and lies

Who are we then, to try to implement ways to test our creator's

strength? Seeking entrance to forbidden places by his sovergnity -

Lest we forget that he paved the way by sacrificing his only

begotten son. So that every agonizing battle we face can be won.

The time has come to re-evaluate our lives:

It's time to reflect

And put God's will for our lives in full effect!!!

I'm Still Standing

Thank you Lord for providing me a safe landing

Even when I wanted to give up - you kept me standing

Though the storms of life constantly brush up against me

I'm still standing

Even when my enemies talked about me

I'm still standing

All the while my friends deserted me

Yet, I'm still standing

Regardless of the loves ones that hurt me

Oh yes, I'm still standing

Through it all - I'm still standing

And no matter what comes my way

I know with God on my side, everything will be alright

And that's is why I can say without a doubt

I'm still standing because my God worked it all out.

GOD'S GRACE

The Grace of God has sustained me

His mercy has kept me

His love has empowered me

To sing praises to his name

The Grace of God has delivered me

His power has healed me

His anointing has enlightened me

To proclaim his goodness everyday

Without his grace, I would be lost

Without his mercy, I would not have been bought

Without his love, I would not be

A sinner saved from my iniquities

Thank God that his grace has sustained me.

FAITH IS

Faith is what you believe

But that you cannot see

Faith is motivation

To excel beyond your wildest dreams

Faith is trusting in God

To bring you through trials and tribulations

Faith is persevering when the pain is overwhelming

Faith is securing your goals with determination

Faith is hope that cast out all doubt

And Faith is definitely knowing that God can work any situation out!!!

YOU CAN MAKE IT

You can make it, no matter how hard it seems

Hold your head up high and hold on to your dreams

Let the negativity pass on by

Embrace adversity with a smile

And believe that God will see you through

Because everything you are facing right now, God will make it worthwhile

Know that trials may come

And the road might get rough

But God is able to pick you back up

Even though you feel all alone

And the pain is overwhelming

Reach up and call out our Savior's name

And he will send his ministering angels

So fret not, for evildoers will be cut down

And you will make it if you put God first and stand your ground.

FORGIVENESS IS THE KEY

How can you forgive someone that has hurt you?

Mistreated, misused, and abused you

Talked about you and left you

Cheated on you and stole from you

The pain is great and it pierces my heart

I am not sure if I can forgive someone that has repeatedly broken my heart.

Yes you can, we all can forgive.

Because, God is the epitome of forgiveness

For He forgave us

And sent his only begotten son, to save us

You know we all have sinned, but God's love for us will never change

And if we are his children, we must exemplify this type of forgiveness just the same

When we sin, we hurt God too

But he never stops blessing us because his love is true

So that is why we must forgive those who have wronged us in any way

Pray for them and do good by them, and God will be with you each and every day!!

GOD CAN

So many of us are going through financial problems

Wondering how you are going to make it through

But God can help you if you trust him and believe that he take care of you

Bills past due, bill collectors calling you

Living from check to check

Barely making due

But God can help you if you trust him and believe that he will bring you through

Trust God in every situation, give him praise

Thank him in advance for the coming of your better days

God wants to bless you, but the enemy wants to destroy you

Take from you, depress and stress you

But God has come that you might have an abundant life

With nothing missing or broken, with unlimited prosperity

Restoring unto you what the enemy has stolen

Because God is Jehovah Jireh, our provider

So know that there is no financial situation that God can't handle

Everything belongs to him, for our Father is rich. And if you trust him and believe in him, God definitely bring you through!!

THE PURPOSE OF THE STORM

There are many times that the waves of life seems to constantly billow

Trial after trial and blow after blow

The nearest safe haven seems so far away

Desperately searching for relief to make it through each day

But even in the storm, there is a sense of calmness that seems near

And that is the Peace of God that erases all doubt and dispels all fear

So why do we fluctuate back and forth with the worldly concerns

Is it because our faith is not strong enough or

Is it just a valuable lesson that we must learn

Well, it is both, you see

We must fight through the pain to see our faith increased

Embrace the challenges of life and chase our dreams

The enemy comes to kill, steal and destroy

But our father has equipped us with bounce back power and everlasting joy

So the next time it begins to rain in your life, don't give in

Instead, tie a knot and hold on, because God has equipped you to win!!!

PURPOSED DESPITE THE PAIN

So many trials and tribulations have come my way

Knocking me flat on my face

Nagging at my heart

And tugging at my dreams

But why does God still have me here when I struggling to endure the pain

Friends turned to enemies

Family turned their back on me too

Barely making ends meet

Raising my kids to be strong

Even though at times, I cry all night long.

Still wondering why God keeps waking me up to fight against this agonizing pain

One day, I questioned God, after decades of struggle and strain

I ask, "God, what is the purpose of all this pain?"

He replied, "My child, you have misunderstood the meaning of the test

And what it means to have faith

It isn't about you; it's all about me preparing you for your predestined place

And even though you have endured a lot, you did not break

So stop questioning my methods, for I make no mistakes

Because in order for you to reach your fullest potential, you must acknowledge all of my ways

For in due season, you will blossom as a new creature filled with spiritual insight

And then and only then will you understand that the pain was purposely inflicted to prepare you for eternal life".

DO WE BELIEVE

We shout

We praise

But do we really believe we can win the race

We fast

We pray

But can we trust God to make a way

We intercede

We testify

But do we praise him only when things are going right

What do you believe, is it only what you can see

Trusting him only for the things he has already made a reality

Or do you really believe in his power

Knowing that his time is not our time

It could takes years, months or merely an hour

What do you believe, do you exercise your faith

Or do you wait anxiously, with doubt in your heart hoping that he makes a way

I believe, that if you trust God and speak his promises over your life

Even when things are not going well,

You can still praise him in advance

You will boast about his goodness to everyone you see

You will gladly thank him for everything that you have already received

Now that's the real evidence that you do believe

AM I BEING USED

Society says that you shouldn't let anyone use you

Now what exactly does that mean?

Didn't God put us here to be used?

To be a blessing to others despite how they treat us

I know, that's a hard pill to swallow

I even have a hard time accepting it myself

Besides, God knows everyone's heart

And if someone wrongs you, he will make them your footstool if you trust him

So stop worrying about being used as long as you are not being misused.

God has given you a specific gift that only you can share with others

Embrace his divine purpose for your life,

And expect abundance and unlimited blessings to overtake your life

HE WOULDN'T ALLOW ME TO GIVE UP

Sometimes, life can be so frustrating

Trying to figure out which way to go

Leaning to my own understanding

Struggling to stay encouraged

When my heart feels so low

But then I realize that God is able

He loves me just the same

Despite my mistakes and faults

He still blesses me anyway

So what makes me so unhappy?

If God has blessed me so

I guess it is because I have not relinquished

complete control

But now I understand

Thank God I Don't Look Like What I've Been Through

That peace comes from giving God all of me

And then I can experience peace on earth

Regardless of all of the negativity

Thank God for his mercy and grace

Thank you Lord for lifting me up

Just when I fell in sorrow

You wouldn't allow me to give up

A Woman of Faith

Yes, I am a woman of Faith

And yes I've made plenty of mistakes

But does that make me any less of a Christian

Because you choose not to erase

The images of sin from my face

Does that make you better than me?

Because we are both in the same race

Racing to a better existence,

Expecting for our blemishes to be covered by grace

Flawed, confused at times, but not misplaced

So how can you judge me?

When we have a common bond that God equates

To being a child of God born into trouble

That only he can judge us

And saves us from destruction

I BELIEVE

I believe in your promises

I believe that you are God

But even though I believe that you are in control

Sometimes doubt creeps into my heart.

I believe in prayer

I believe that you will see me through

I have to keep reminding myself of this very thing,

Because Satan is seeking my attention too

I believe that I am blessed

I believe that I can win

And as long as I believe in God

I will always experience his abundant blessings!!!!

SUCCESS IS MY NAME

Success is my name

Despite my current mistakes

I can still rise again.

Sometimes my friends and family let me down

Sometimes I feel that I have lost my way

I wanted to just give up

But I awoke the next day

It must be a reason

Some purpose that I have overlooked

Although I am not sure of what it could be

I know that with everything I've been through

I could probably write a book.

But regardless of the negativity that I once embraced

I am ready to give this positivity thing a chance

I mean, what could happen.

I have already experienced the worst

I guess it could only get better if I believe in me first.

So I am saying good riddings to peer pressure, anxiety, anger and fear

Thank God I Don't Look Like What I've Been Through

Hello love, joy, peace and a fresh start with great expectations for the rest of this year

I realize now, that the only one that can keep me down is myself

Can't blame anyone else for the choices I made

It's time for me to accept full responsibility for my life and change

I can be anything I want to be

There are no limitations, no shackles binding me

And so, my name is Success

I am a Doctor, a Lawyer, Engineer and Teacher

I am a Congressman, Policewoman, Professor and Leader

And yes, I realize that once I change for the better, I might lose friends

But a friend is someone that wants to see you succeed, not encourages you to sin

I can't stop now, I have done all that I know to do

And where I am today, I choose to be the new and improve

So, don't get it twisted, I still keep it real and I am definitely down

But the only difference is Success is my name and I am down with turning my life around.

I ALMOST GAVE UP

I almost gave up

Life just didn't seem fair

Bad break after bad break

Negativity everywhere

I just wanted a beacon of hope

Just a small sparkle of light

To signal that better days were coming

If I just continued to do what was right

But the weariness set in motion

I began to doubt my deliverance

The more I pressed forward

The more things shook my existence

I was at my last attempt

To fight the good fight of faith

When God spoke these words

"Follow me; I am the truth and the life"

I picked my head up from my lap

And reach toward heaven's door

Thank God I Don't Look Like What I've Been Through

And just as I called out to God

I felt the chains of bondage hit the floor

I guess I forgot to use my power

The power of calling on his name

For him I am so very grateful

Because he didn't allow me to give into my pain

I AM HEALED

I am healed

I am free

No more pain ailing me

I am healed

I am free

I received my healing spiritually

I am healed

I am free

God's plan for my life …I receive

I am healed

I am free

Thank you Lord….for continuously blessing me

LOOKING FOR LOVE

Everyone wants to be loved

Held and cherished

Spending time together and laughing

But every time I look for someone

I get discouraged

Maybe I am looking for love in all the wrong places

Tricked by hidden agendas lurking behind smiling faces

But what do I do

Time is running out

I'm getting older by the minute

Finding love for me has probably run out

Searching for a companion and not really understanding myself

What is wrong with me?

Do I need some relationship help?

And then I decided to pray like never before seeking God's voice

And what he told me made me change my course

"Young lady, he said, I have orchestrated every detail of your life

And there is nothing wrong with you

I am just preparing you to be a wife.

You are far more precious than you portray, so I blocked those unworthy men

Instead, I have been working behind the scenes to send you a husband that will love you until the end

So stop searching for love because that is not your rightful place

You deserve to be pursued

Because I never intended for you to chase

Remember Naomi and how she found true love seeking me first

And why would I not do it for you….for I have no respector of persons

I tell you that it's a must to love yourself first, and seek me in everything you do

And in due season…..your Boaz… I will introduce to you".

GOD IS MY SOURCE

God is my source

Not my job or my spouse

God is always behind the scenes working it out

God is my source

Not friends in high places

Or those smiling in my face

Instead it is the Grace of God that keeps me

God is my source

Not the money in the bank

My wealthy family heritage

Or my notoriety in the community

But God that has blessed me

God is my source

Need I say more?

I been through enough situations to know

Where my help cometh from

I seen too much to doubt were my provision comes from

I have risen from my sleep too many times to not know where my health and strength comes from

I declare, I decree, I profess and I believe that no matter what society may think

I know without a doubt that God is my source!!!

Words of Wisdom: FINDING YOUR HOPE AGAIN

- **JEREMIAH 3:15**

  And I will give you pastors according to mine heart, which shall feed you with knowledge and understanding.

FINDING YOUR HOPE AGAIN

Over the years, I have been privileged to be empowered by so many wonderful vessels for the Lord. And I wanted to share their spiritual wisdom with you as well. So often we can get bogged down by life itself. We seem to forget where our help cometh from. We tend to feel that all hope is gone. But thank God, for even though we may fall, we can always get back up again if we believe!!!!

You see, sometimes just some encouraging words can lift you out of the dumps of depression. It can come from anyone at anytime anywhere. God is universal and he is ever present!!! He will never fail us even when we feel that we have fallen beyond our desires.

Thus, on the preceding pages, there are responses from the desk of a few of God's chosen vessels that so graciously provided some words of encouragement when we are faced with ***losing all hope***. I pray that God has his way and something that is spoken from their spiritual perspective gives you hope, peace and a sound mind as God works things out in your favor!!

Stay Encouraged & Be blessed

Tanya ShawTyus

FROM THEIR DESK TO YOUR HEARTS

Minister Ricky Taylor
Greater Community Church of Chattanooga, COGIC
Chattanooga, TN

There is so much I can say ha-ha.......Paul says in Romans 5:5 " And hope does not disappoint us, because God has poured out his love into our hearts by the Holy Spirit, whom he has given us." Jeremiah 29:11 "For I know the plans I have for you declares The Lord, plans to prosper you and not to harm you, plans to give you a hope and a future."

So for someone who has lost hope, I would tell them that God loves you unconditionally and it doesn't matter how imperfect you've been. You may have experienced insurmountable circumstances and disappointments but God is merciful and He

still has a greater plan for your life. You must understand that all things work together for the good of those who are called according to his purpose Romans 8:28. God's plan for your life will supersede your expectations!!!! Keep the faith, keep believing.....
And don't tap out because God is working it out!!!!

===

Pastor Rev. Wayne Smith
Pilgrim Rest Baptist Church
Jackson, TN

How do you bring light into a gloomy and dark filled life. One of the greatest skills/ tools that I try to employ is that of attentive listening. In doing so I learn the cause which one has allowed to come in and conquer and bound them into a mindset of total hopelessness. My words are carefully chosen with the aid of the Holy Spirit, to assist them to climb to a higher level. Getting one who is in such a low state of mind, to open their mind to a different way of thinking is never an easy task.

One has to become aware of the positive values which they have already accomplished and that have been a great inspiration to others. Then help them to see that they can do all things through Christ who strengthens them (Philippians 4:13). When we put our trust and faith in God and stop relying on our own abilities then we become successful. Remember we are not the one who made us but God himself (Psalms 100:3), and he has something special for you. You must remember that you are wonderfully made (Psalms 139:14), that you are an heir to God's Kingdom (Galatians 4:7), that the earth is the Lords and the fullness there of the world and all that dwell therein (Psalms 24:1). **You must focus on the positive and step out on faith!!!!**

===

Pastor Luke Steven Hall
New Vision Christian Church
Forest Park, GA
www.nvcc3.org

Hope is easily lost when it's placed in someone or something that wasn't created to sustain it. You must first understand that your hope is not gone, but simply misplaced. The bible says in Romans 15:13, May the God of hope fill you with all joy and peace in believing, so that by the power of the Holy Spirit you may abound in hope."

Even in your lowest moments, you must member that you control where you put your hope, and the picture that you paint on the canvass of your imagination, will one day hang on the wall of your reality!!! *The songwriter said it best when he said, "My hope is built on nothing less, than Jesus' blood and righteousness"*

===

Pastor Boris Hall
Founder & Senior Leader of Exousia I.N.C
Forest Park, GA

Hope

The world's definition: 1. the feeling that what is wanted can be had or that events will turn out for the best:

God's definition: 2. Expectation of a divinely provided future.

Praise the Lord my brothers and sisters,

I know the pressures of life can be overwhelming sometimes, I also know how it feels to reach a place of hopelessness. I will say to you what God said to me in my time of trouble, He said, "I have not forgotten about you". That's right, He has seen every tear and heard every cry, you're not alone.

Above are two definitions of hope, the first is how the world defines hope, notice it says "the feeling that what is wanted can be had", the world operates by what they feel, the enemy tries to make you ""feel" that God has forsaken you, that you can't make it, he tells you that you will never be anything, that you'll never reach the promised places in your life. But God, in His definition of hope says that "it is a Devine expectation of a provided future", notice He says that He is going to provide and that we should expect it. Jeremiah 29:11 says, " For I know the thoughts I that I think toward you, says the Lord, thoughts of peace and not of evil, to give you a future and a hope."

So hold on my brother and my sister, God knows the plans He has for you, even in your present situation, in the midst of your tears

He still has a plan, and if you faint not He's going to deliver you. **I will end with this, I've never seen the righteous forsaken, I've seen them cry, I've seen them go through hell, I've seen them fall and get back up again, but I've never seen them forsaken, be blessed and know that you are the righteous!!!.**

Prophetess Chavon and I are praying for you that your faith fail not and we love you.

==

Minister Johnny Fitzhugh II
Cypress Creek Baptist Church (under the leadership of Pastor Clifford E. Wynn Jr.)
Selmer, TN

What do you say to someone who is looking for hope?

I have had moments in my life were I have unknowingly diminished my faith by magnifying the problem that was designed for me to overcome. **Hebrews 11:1 states that FAITH IS.....the substance of things hope for and the evidence of things not seen.** *What I had to realize was that although my issues and circumstances were visible, the God we serve is invincible and able to rearrange our vision to see that same problem as a stepping stone. And this stepping stone will be the* **catalyst** *that draws us closer to God's purpose being fulfilled in our life instead of a stumbling block.*

Thus, I would like to inform my brother or my sister that what you are going through is designed and pre-planned by God to work for your good (Romans 8:28)!!! Therefore, be encouraged my brother or my sister, for the tribulations of the present time cannot compare to the Glory that is to come!!!

I love you and God loves you more!!! Be blessed!!!

===

SCRIPTURES FOR EVERY NEED:

A LIFE TOOL

- **MATTHEW 4:4**

Jesus answered, "It is written: "Man does not live on bread alone, but on every word that comes from the mouth of God".

SCRIPTURES TO LIVE BY

✝ *1 Corinthians 10:13:* There hath no temptation taken you but such as is common to man: but God is faithful, who will not suffer you to be tempted above that ye are able; but will with the temptation also make a way to escape, that ye may be able to bear it.

✝ *1 Corinthians 16:13: Watch ye, stand fast in the faith, quit you like men, be strong.*

✝ *1 John 1:9: If we confess our sins, he is faithful and just to forgive us our sins, and to cleanse us from all unrighteousness.*

✝ *1 Peter 4:12-13: Beloved, think it not strange concerning the fiery trial which is to try you, as though some strange thing happened unto you. But rejoice, inasmuch as ye are partakers of Christ's sufferings; that, when his glory shall be revealed, ye may be glad also with exceeding joy.*

✝ *1Peter 5:7: Casting all your care upon him; for he careth for you.*

✝ *2 Corinthians 4:16-18: For which cause we faint not; but though our outward man perish, yet the inward man is renewed day by day. For our light affliction, which is but for a moment, worketh for us a far more exceeding and eternal weight of glory; While we look not at the things which are seen, but at the things which are not seen: for the things which are seen are temporal; but the things which are not seen are eternal.*

✝ *2 Timothy 1:7: For God hath not given us the spirit of fear; but of power, and of love, and of a sound mind.*

- ✝ *Acts 18:10: For I am with thee, and no man shall set on thee to hurt thee: for I have much people in this city.*

- ✝ *Colossians 3:23: And whatsoever ye do, do it heartily, as to the Lord, and not unto men;*

- ✝ *Deuteronomy 31:6: Be strong and of a good courage, fear not, nor be afraid of them: for the LORD thy God, he it is that doth go with thee; he will not fail thee, nor forsake thee.*

- ✝ *Ephesians 2:8: For by grace are ye saved through faith; and that not of yourselves: it is the gift of God: Not of works, lest any man should boast. For we are his workmanship, created in Christ Jesus unto good works, which God hath before ordained that we should walk in them.*

- ✝ *Ephesians 3:20: Now unto him that is able to do exceeding abundantly above all that we ask or think, according to the power that worketh in us*

- ✝ *Ephesians 6:10: Finally, my brethren, be strong in the Lord, and in the power of his might.*

- ✝ *Galatians 5:22-23: But the fruit of the Spirit is love, joy, peace, longsuffering, gentleness, goodness, faith, Meekness, temperance: against such there is no law.*

- ✝ *Hebrew 11:1: 1Now faith is the substance of things hoped for, the evidence of things not seen.*

- ✝ *Hebrew 11:6: But without faith it is impossible to please him: for he that cometh to God must believe that he is, and that he is a rewarder of them that diligently seek him.*

- ✝ *Hebrew 12:2: Looking unto Jesus the author and finisher of our faith; who for the joy that was set before him endured the cross, despising the shame, and is set down at the right hand of the throne of God.*

- ☦ *Hebrew 4:16:* Let us therefore come boldly unto the throne of grace that we may obtain mercy, and find grace to help in time of need.

- ☦ *Isaiah 26:3:* Thou wilt keep him in perfect peace, whose mind is stayed on thee: because he trusteth in thee.

- ☦ *Isaiah 40:29:* He giveth power to the faint; and to them that have no might he increaseth strength.

- ☦ *Isaiah 40:31:* But they that wait upon the LORD shall renew their strength; they shall mount up with wings as eagles; they shall run, and not be weary; and they shall walk, and not faint.

- ☦ *Isaiah 41:10:* Fear thou not; for I am with thee: be not dismayed; for I am thy God: I will strengthen thee; yea, I will help thee; yea, I will uphold thee with the right hand of my righteousness.

- ☦ *Isaiah 54:17:* No weapon that is formed against thee shall prosper; and every tongue that shall rise against thee in judgment thou shalt condemn. This is the heritage of the servants of the LORD, and their righteousness is of me, saith the LORD.

- ☦ *Isaiah 55:8:* For my thoughts are not your thoughts, neither are your ways my ways, saith the LORD.

- ☦ *James 1:12:* Blessed is the man that endureth temptation: for when he is tried, he shall receive the crown of life, which the Lord hath promised to them that love him

- ☦ *.James 1:2-4:* My brethren, count it all joy when ye fall into divers temptations; Knowing this, that the trying of your faith worketh patience. But let patience have her perfect work, that ye may be perfect and entire, wanting nothing.

- ☦ *James 1:17:* Every good gift and every perfect gift is from above, and cometh down from the Father of lights, with whom is no variableness, neither shadow of turning.

Thank God I Don't Look Like What I've Been Through

- ✞ *James 1:5-6: If any of you lack wisdom, let him ask of God, that giveth to all men liberally, and upbraideth not; and it shall be given him. But let him ask in faith, nothing wavering. For he that wavereth is like a wave of the sea driven with the wind and tossed.*

- ✞ *James 4:15: For that ye ought to say, If the Lord will, we shall live, and do this, or that.*

- ✞ *Jeremiah 29:11: For I know the thoughts that I think toward you, saith the LORD, thoughts of peace, and not of evil, to give you an expected end.*

- ✞ *Joel 2:25: And I will restore to you the years that the locust hath eaten, the cankerworm, and the caterpiller, and the palmerworm, my great army which I sent among you.*

- ✞ *John 10:10: The thief cometh not, but for to steal, and to kill, and to destroy: I am come that they might have life, and that they might have it more abundantly.*

- ✞ *John 14:27: Peace I leave with you, my peace I give unto you: not as the world giveth, give I unto you. Let not your heart be troubled, neither let it be afraid.*

- ✞ *John 14:6: Jesus saith unto him, I am the way, the truth, and the life: no man cometh unto the Father, but by me.*

- ✞ *John 16:33: These things I have spoken unto you, that in me ye might have peace. In the world ye shall have tribulation: but be of good cheer; I have overcome the world.*

- ✞ *John 3:16: For God so loved the world, that he gave his only begotten Son, that whosoever believeth in him should not perish, but have everlasting life.*

- ✞ *John 5:24: Verily, verily, I say unto you, He that heareth my word, and believeth on him that sent me, hath everlasting life, and shall not come into condemnation; but is passed from death unto life.*

- ✞ *Joshua 1:9: Have not I commanded thee? Be strong and of a good courage; be not afraid, neither be thou dismayed: for the LORD thy God is with thee whithersoever thou goest.*

- ✞ *Lamentations 3:22-23: It is of the LORD'S mercies that we are not consumed, because his compassions fail not. They are new every morning: great is thy faithfulness.*

- ✞ *Matthew 11:28-30: Come unto me, all ye that labour and are heavy laden, and I will give you rest. Take my yoke upon you, and learn of me; for I am meek and lowly in heart: and ye shall find rest unto your souls. For my yoke is easy, and my burden is light.*

- ✞ *Matthew 28:18: And Jesus came and spake unto them, saying, All power is given unto me in heaven and in earth.*

- ✞ *Matthew 6:33:* But seek ye first the kingdom of God, and his righteousness; and all these things shall be added unto you.

- ✞ *Nahum 1:7: The LORD is good, a strong hold in the day of trouble; and he knoweth them that trust in him.*

- ✞ *Philippians 1:6: Being confident of this very thing, that he which hath begun a good work in you will perform it until the day of Jesus Christ:*

- ✞ *Philippians 4:13: I can do all things through Christ which strengtheneth me.*

- ✞ *Philippians 4:19: But my God shall supply all your need according to his riches in glory by Christ Jesus.*

- ✞ *Philippians 4:6-7: Be careful for nothing; but in every thing by prayer and supplication with thanksgiving let your requests be made known unto God. And the peace of God, which passeth all understanding, shall keep your hearts and minds through Christ Jesus.*

✞ *Philippians 4:8: Finally, brethren, whatsoever things are true, whatsoever things are honest, whatsoever things are just, whatsoever things are pure, whatsoever things are lovely, whatsoever things are of good report; if there be any virtue, and if there be any praise, think on these things.*

✞ *Proverbs 18:10: The name of the LORD is a strong tower: the righteous runneth into it, and is safe.*

✞ *Proverbs 24:16: For a just man falleth seven times, and riseth up again: but the wicked shall fall into mischief.*

✞ *Proverbs 3:5-6: Trust in the LORD with all thine heart; and lean not unto thine own understanding.*

✞ *Psalms 119:28: My soul melteth for heaviness: strengthen thou me according unto thy word.*

✞ *Psalms 120:1: In my distress I cried unto the LORD, and he heard me.*

✞ *Psalms 16:8: I have set the LORD always before me: because he is at my right hand, I shall not be moved.*

✞ *Psalms 20:4: Grant thee according to thine own heart, and fulfil all thy counsel.*

✞ *Psalms 34:18: The LORD is nigh unto them that are of a broken heart; and saveth such as be of a contrite spirit.*

✞ *Psalms 34:8: O taste and see that the LORD is good: blessed is the man that trusteth in him.*

- *Psalms 37:1: Fret not thyself because of evildoers, neither be thou envious against the workers of iniquity.*

- *Psalms 37:4: Delight thyself also in the LORD; and he shall give thee the desires of thine heart.*

- *Psalms 37:25: I have been young, and now am old; yet have I not seen the righteous forsaken, nor his seed begging bread.*

- *Psalms 46:1: God is our refuge and strength, a very present help in trouble.*

- *Psalms 55:16: As for me, I will call upon God; and the LORD shall save me.*
- *Psalms 91:11: For he shall give his angels charge over thee, to keep thee in all thy ways.*

- *Revelation 21:4: And God shall wipe away all tears from their eyes; and there shall be no more death, neither sorrow, nor crying, neither shall there be any more pain: for the former things are passed away.*

- *Romans 5:8: But God commendeth his love toward us, in that, while we were yet sinners, Christ died for us.*

- *Romans 8:28: And we know that all things work together for good to them that love God, to them who are the called according to his purpose.*

- *Romans 8:31: What shall we then say to these things? If God be for us, who can be against us?*

- *Romans 8:37: Nay, in all these things we are more than conquerors through him that loved us.*

- *Romans 8:38-39: For I am persuaded, that neither death, nor life, nor angels, nor principalities, nor powers, nor things present, nor things to come, nor height, nor depth, nor any other creature, shall be able to separate us from the love of God, which is in Christ Jesus our Lord.*

Thank God I Don't Look Like What I've Been Through

- ✞ *If you don't remember anything else, remember that everything you go through serves a purpose!!!*
- ✞ *You are here for a reason!!!!*
- ✞ *You can be victorious!!!*
- ✞ *Your faith activates your destiny!!!!*
- ✞ *And most importantly always give God thanks!!!*
- ✞ *Thank him for waking you up!!!*
- ✞ *Thank him for your friends and family!!*
- ✞ *Thank him for provision and divine protection!!!*
- ✞ *And thank him because you don't look like what you've been through!!!!!*

God is good and He is able!!!

Be blessed and definitely encouraged!!!

Tanya Shaw Tyus

FOR PERSONAL REFLECTION

NOTES

For Personal Reflection

NOTES

ABOUT THE AUTHOR

Tanya Shaw Tyus is a native from Brownsville, Tennessee. Having accomplished many feats, writing and motivational speaking has been her forte. She also has a vast amount of experience in other areas from the business arena to the educational field. A self-motivated motivational leader that has managed to make the best better. She enjoys working with youth and as a result has started her own outreach: T.A.N.A (takinganewapproach.com). This indeed makes Tanya Shaw Tyus worthy of the testimonies she proclaims. To her, being blessed is not just a statement....it's a lifestyle!!!

www.ingramcontent.com/pod-product-compliance
Lightning Source LLC
LaVergne TN
LVHW051608070426
835507LV00021B/2838